Penguin Books
China After Mao: 'Seek Truth From Facts'
by Liu Heung Shing

Liu Heung Shing was born in Hong Kong in 1951. Three years later, he returned to China, settling in Fuzhou in the southeastern province of Fujian. There he received his early education, moving back to Hong Kong in 1962 to attend high school. In 1971, Liu enrolled at New York City's Hunter College where he studied political science and journalism.

He was first introduced to photography in his final year at the college in a course taught by renowned *Life* magazine photographer, Gjon Mili. His childhood exposure to drawing and painting enhanced his understanding and enthusiasm for photography, and in 1976, following his graduation from Hunter College, he became Mili's apprentice. During this unique experience, Liu was deeply influenced by Mili's editorial and aesthetic ideas.

In 1976, Liu began working for *Time* magazine on assignments in China, starting with a story on the death of Mao. Five years later, he joined The Associated Press, and now travels extensively through China, writing as well as photographing for AP.

To My Mother and Father

The choice of photographs in this book is entirely my own. It was made with only one thought in mind — to show how the world's most populous country is recovering from a decade of human catastrophe (1966-76) to reassert itself and meet the arduous challenges of modernization. In short, this is a visual record of how people live in post-Mao China.

I want to thank all those who generously offered me their help and encouragement — particularly Victoria Graham, who wrote the introductions accompanying each chapter. She was and still is my most enthusiastic supporter, both as my bureau chief in Peking and as a frequent traveling colleague in China. Her zest for human-interest stories and acute appreciation of visual images influenced and complemented my own efforts. She was at my side when many of the photographs in this book were taken.

Thanks to my editor, Neal Ulevich, for his timely rescues of photographic supplies which had to be flown from Tokyo to Peking, and his great enthusiasm for China; to my agent and friend, Robert Pledge, for his interest in my work; to Mike Morrow for inspiring me over the years to do this book; to my former journalistic colleagues in Peking, John Roderick, Richard Bernstein and Fox Butterfield, for sharing with me their considerable knowledge and experience of China, and for their encouragement as well; to my Chinese friends, who prefer to remain anonymous, but without whose help and cooperation many of these photographs could not have been taken, and to Foreign Affairs officials throughout the country who, with but a few exceptions, helped to make my work easier.

I greatly appreciate the understanding and support of Mr Keith Fuller, president and general manager of The Associated Press, who first posted me to Peking. Thanks also to Harold Buell, AP vice president for newsphotos, for his generous moral support during the project, and to Arnold Drapkin of *Time* magazine for sending me to China in the early years.

Last but not least, special acknowledgment goes to Chesca Long-Innes for her skillful editing and to Chumpon Apisuk who traveled all the way to Peking to get a feel for China before he set out to design the book.

PENGUIN BOOKS

CHINA AFTER MAO:
'SEEK TRUTH FROM FACTS'

LIU HEUNG SHING

"Practice is the sole criterion of truth." Calligraphy by Bai Hua.
This phrase from a controversial essay by Nanjing University professor Hu Fuming, sanctioned by Deng Xiaoping at the Third Plenum of the 11th Party Congress in 1978, has since become the basis for the guiding slogan of post-Mao leadership: "Seek truth from facts."

Penguin Books Ltd, Harmondsworth, Middlesex, England
Penguin Books, 40 West 23rd Street, New York, New York 10010, U.S.A.
Penguin Books Australia Ltd, Ringwood, Victoria, Australia
Penguin Books Canada Ltd, 2801 John Street, Markham, Ontario, Canada L3R 1B4
Penguin Books (N.Z.) Ltd, 182-190 Wairau Road, Auckland 10, New Zealand

First published 1983

Produced in Hong Kong by Asia 2000 Ltd.
6th Floor, 146 Prince Edward Road West
Kowloon

Photographs and captions by Liu Heung Shing
Chapter introductions by Victoria Graham

Design by Chumpon Apisuk
Cover design by Margaret Ng
Calligraphy by Bai Hua

Coordinating editor: Chesca Long-Innes
Production editor: Adi Ignatius

Printed in Hong Kong by Ying Wai Printing Press
Photoset in English Times, headlines in Estella by
Eliza Fong, Asia 2000 Ltd.

CONTENTS

INTRODUCTION

This collection of photographs by Liu Heung Shing is the truest, most profound photographic portrayal of China since the communists took over the country more than three decades ago.

Hundreds of photographers with fine eyes and marvelous skills have been to China to shoot tens of thousands of pictures. Like most foreigners in general, they stay for only a few days or a few weeks. They travel under the guidance of the China Travel Service or they wander the streets on their own and shoot what it is easiest to see: rows of adorable schoolchildren, minority tribesmen in their colorful costumes, sturdy peasants tilling the fields, great rows of Chinese massing through the streets of one or another of the country's cities. In the vast majority of cases, the result has stressed the image itself, photography, while keeping an understanding of China in second place.

If a certain calendar picture image of China has emerged from this, it would have been difficult to expect otherwise in a country where most people go for only short visits, where they do not speak the language and where their destinations are chosen, not by themselves, but by Chinese officialdom itself.

Liu's pictures leap beyond the cliché to show China as it is. Taken together, his photographs are a comprehensive, subtle, unsentimental, unsparingly honest mosaic of Chinese society. He has photographed the country in all of its moods, in all of its seasons, from the grasslands of Inner Mongolia to the coasts of Guangdong Province to the interiors of subtropical Yunnan. Equally important, he brings a knowledge and experience to his subject that no other photographer possesses. He is, after all, Chinese. He speaks three dialects of the Chinese language — Fujianese, Cantonese and Mandarin, the standard dialect. And while by no means an outsider to China, he is at the same time a bridge between China and the west.

In the 19th century, pioneers like John Thomson recorded the photographic images for future generations. In the 1930's and 1940's there was Henri Cartier-Bresson. For the post-Mao period, now there is Liu Heung Shing.

For nearly two years, Liu was *Time* magazine's photographer in China (1979-80). Through the magazine, through syndications of his work to other publications, and through various additional assignments that he took on, Liu took the majority of the pictures that made their way into western publications during that time.

To a great extent, Liu has uncovered a China that is in the process of uncovering itself; he shows us a society emerging from a frightening period of political terror into an era where its true essence could be expressed once again. More specifically, he shows us a China that is emerging from the era of Mao into an as yet undefined, but somehow more hopeful future.

The earliest pictures in this collection were taken in 1976, after the death of Mao. In the last years of Mao's reign, particularly during the so-called Cultural Revolution, China had been crushed by an extremist political tyranny. The Cultural Revolution itself, which lasted officially from 1966 until 1976, began as an effort by Mao to get rid of those in the leadership who threatened not only his absolute power, but also his romantic, extremely egalitarian view of society.

During the movement China was swept away into sheer, frightening madness. Universities were closed down for three years or more. Churches and temples were destroyed. Love was attacked as bourgeois sentimentality. All private enterprise and free markets were branded "capitalist" and closed down. Cultural life was reduced to a handful of model ballets and operas and a dozen or so "revolutionary" songs. A cult of the personality, unseen in the world since the days of Stalin, raged around the figure of Mao himself. Wherever the visitor went in the entire country, and no matter whom one talked to, people spoke in political clichés, using the few phrases, mostly glorifications of Mao, that could not land them in trouble.

In the years after Mao's death, however, the far more pragmatic leadership, while still very authoritarian by international standards, loosened its controls considerably. People gradually realized that they did not have to mouth political slogans anymore, that they could start to be themselves. Such personal matters as love, religion and style emerged from their decade-long suppression. Private markets reappeared as did diverse aspects of Chinese society such as Buddhist pilgrims, traditional art, Chinese opera, western music, and among an impatient urban youth, demands for more and more political freedom.

At the same time, the extreme adoration of Mao was declared a mistake. The late Chairman faded into the background as most people concerned themselves with the trials and joys of ordinary life. And so, on page 33, we have Liu's wonderful picture of a shopkeeper eating a bowl of rice while above him, entirely forgotten, partially concealed behind some old shoes, is a tattered portrait of Mao. The picture is one of my favorites. It is the perfect emblem of a country that is returning to itself.

China, in these pictures, is poor and often dilapidated, a simple journalistic truth frequently absent from the work of those photographers who are seeking only to use China as the raw material for magnificent images. The country is lean and spare. It is filled with human character but physically it is dull, drab, unadorned. Liu's photography has captured this entire country undisguised, unposed, authentic, complex, unique, glancing without advance notice into the lens, and frozen there for eternity.

In decades to come, we and those who follow us will need to look back on post-Maoist China and try to understand what was the experience then of the nearly one quarter of humanity that is Chinese. It will, I predict, be the images in this collection by Liu Heung Shing that, more than any other single source, will most deeply touch our understanding.

Richard Bernstein, May 1983

Richard Bernstein was Peking correspondent for *Time* magazine from 1980-82, and is the author of *From the Center of the Earth: The Search for the Truth About China*.

FOREWORD

In the spring of 1976, I went to work for my photographic mentor, Gjon Mili, with whom I had studied photojournalism. I spent many memorable afternoons during the months that followed poring over the negatives, contact sheets and transparencies of Mili's lifetime of work, helping him to prepare a book of his photographs.

I can't recall any moment that Gjon made mention of apertures, cameras or depths of field. More important than technical photographic skills, Gjon taught me how to interpret human experiences and capture them in two-dimensional images with warmth. And he instilled in me the belief that one must care deeply about one's subject matter.

When I came to China with my first assignment for *Time* magazine, I never reached my destination of Peking, where I was to photograph the impending state funeral of China's "Great Helmsman," Mao Tse-tung. Stranded in Canton, I was informed by my travel service guide that a visit to Peking at the time was "inconvenient." I rushed out to the streets, and for the next couple of days photographed people preparing local funeral ceremonies for Mao.

I sensed an unusual calm on the faces of what normally are the most volatile people in China, the Cantonese. I wasn't sure what to make of it. Were they really saddened by the death of Mao, whose quotations they had so religiously memorized? Or were they relieved by his death and concerned with where their futures would lie?

I have since learned that Mao's death was a long-awaited shock for the quarter of mankind, the one billion Chinese. It has taken the people longer than they expected to recover from that shock; to re-think the future without Mao, and to undo what Mao had idealistically but relentlessly imposed on them.

I returned to China for many more professional visits, each lasting a few weeks to a few months. But I soon realized that it would take much longer to understand China, with its complex history and the enormous impact politics has on its people and institutions. And that to photograph the country and reveal it in images, I would have to establish personal relationships and be more patient than the Chinese themselves.

I took up residence in the fall of 1979 as a Time photographer, and later joined the staff of The Associated Press. Speaking the Chinese language and a couple of provincial dialects does, of course, make work easier for me than other photographers — but not much. Journalistic freedom is highly circumscribed in a country where the system keeps foreigners on the periphery of important events. However, I have never encountered any government censorship of my outgoing reports and wirephoto transmissions. And in China, we are free to question and reject the information we receive. This, to me, is the true barometer for freedom of the press.

The relations I have established over the years with my official Chinese colleagues are good and amicable. We are quite far apart, though, in the realm of aesthetic interpretation. And we differ greatly in our conception of what makes a good photograph.

In August 1979, while covering former US Vice-President Mondale's visit for *Time,* I went to a Peking cloisonné factory with Mrs Mondale and her daughter. While preparing to photograph the Mondales as they browsed for souvenirs, I saw through my viewfinder a hand reaching out to try and arrange an ashtray on top of the glass case in front of them.

I looked over my shoulder and saw the Xinhua (New China News Agency) photographer. His aesthetic judgment greatly disturbed by the ashtray, he finally couldn't resist removing it. Then he snapped the picture with a strobe mounted on his Rollei-120.

Many Chinese photographers, like my Xinhua colleague, believe a photograph ought to be conceived as a traditional Chinese landscape painting. Chinese photography owes much of its aesthetic to the Taoist concept of harmonies between man and nature. The Xinhua photographer must have thought the ashtray upset the otherwise balanced photograph, so he eliminated it.

Early one January morning in Peking, Xinhua bookstores put on sale *The Selected Works of Liu Shaoqi,* China's late president persecuted by the radical followers of Mao for his pragmatic economic policies. I went to the Xinhua store in Wangfujing, hoping to photograph people buying Liu's books. More than an hour had gone by with no customers while I hung around the dimly lit counter specially set up for the sale. There was simply a lack of interest in this sort of book.

The next morning the Communist Party's organ, *People's Daily,* was fronted with a Xinhua photograph showing a large crowd buying Liu's selected works. The photograph was taken in the same store where I had waited in vain. I have no doubt how my Xinhua colleagues did it. This time, instead of removing the ashtray, one of them arranged a crowd around the counter and clicked.

A visit to the Meigukou coal mine in Shanxi Province also shed light on the Chinese perception of what is suitable to photograph. I was photographing the Chinese coalminers, whose faces were covered with coal dust, when a cadre voiced objection: "Please, the coalminers prefer not to be photographed like this. They don't look clean." As if the Chinese coalminers were the only ones in the world who looked unwashed from having to work 650 meters underground, the cadre advised me to photograph them after they had showered.

In China, official tours rarely reveal spontaneous situations. Frequently factory workers and peasants are told to take days off to clean up their workplaces and prepare them for visits by foreign guests. I am reminded of this whenever I see signs that say, "Warmly welcome American friends."

In the winter of 1981, I visited Harbin, a rugged industrial city in the fertile plain of northeastern Heilongjiang, a province that shares a 3,400-kilometer border with the Soviet Union, China's arch rival. On the way to the airport I met about 100 peasants following a row of tractors, each wearing a pair of "punk" reflective sunglasses. Waving large paper fans, they were cheering and dancing, celebrating the traditional Lunar New Year. The Party secretary of the Pioneer Brigade was eager to have me photograph the joyous peasant performers with their rosy cheeks and painted lips, but he insisted that I wait until the group had been arranged in proper order. "Never mind," I said, "it's more candid this way." "What are candid pictures?" he asked, standing in front of my Leica, in a friendly way.

It couldn't be a more mistaken idea to think that the Chinese are hostile to photography. I have never seen any people with so little who would spend such significant portions of their low salaries to have their pictures taken. At the Forbidden City, the Great Wall, or the Temple of Heaven, thousands of Chinese tourists pose for pictures every day. In a photo shop manned by unemployed educated youths in Peking Station on the local subway, commuters pay 30 fen (18 cents US) to have their pictures taken in front of a train. And a local photographic studio with its two tungsten light stands even provides props for portraits — handbags and plastic flowers for ladies, suits and ties for men.

Socially, it has been possible for me to make friends with Chinese photographers, but not easy. I once invited four *China Daily* photographers to my flat for a meal, and to discuss a photo project. One of them said he would have to consult his editor before the invitation could be accepted. A week later he rang me to say we'd better meet somewhere other than in my home.

The exception is rare, but it does exist. I met another Chinese photographer on the set of "Marco Polo," and invited him too for a meal at my home. He said, "With pleasure." I discovered, as we became good friends, that he was the son of a powerful minister of the State Council, China's cabinet.

It is of course impossible to capture the Chinese in a single photograph. But it is hoped that, viewed together, the following pages will provide a glimpse of the people in post-Mao China. The Chinese have survived poverty for two millenia. But the hope and pride which the Chinese communists restored in China when they gained power in 1949 has since almost been lost in the ensuing incessant political campaigns and social upheavals.

Yet, though the nation is still trapped in its own deeply rooted feudal traditions, it is at the same time protected by the richness of its civilization. As if completely undaunted by past adversities, a Chinese man in his forties, whose father played a significant role in introducing communism to China, recounted for me, one by one, all the political movements and campaigns of the past few decades. When he had finished, I counted 25 in the 33-year history of the People's Republic.

Westerners are puzzled. "What kind of people," they ask themselves, "could endure the aftermaths and persecutions of 'education' and 're-education,' 'criticism' and 'self-criticism' year after year?" The answer is, the Chinese.

Liu Heung Shing

POLITICS

For 2,000 years China was ruled by an emperor, the "Son of Heaven," and then for many years by Chairman Mao Tse-tung, who was called "the Sun." Today China is ruled by a gerontocracy of revolutionaries, veterans of the Long March, many of whom bear the scars of political battles and persecution by the patriarchal Mao and the radical "Gang of Four." At the helm is the pragmatic and visionary Deng Xiaoping, purged twice by Mao and the radicals for his attempts to check their mania, correct their blunders and modernize China.

Virtually everyone in power today was disgraced at one time or another during the Cultural Revolution, which lasted from 1966 to 1976. In 1981, however, Deng and his followers mustered enough support to put Mao's widow, Jiang Qing, and the rest of the "Gang" on trial. She was condemned to death, but, for the sake of political stability, the sentence was later commuted to life imprisonment. The undisputed triumvirate of 1983 is led by Deng, a man who has shed titles but held on to power, Premier Zhao Ziyang, economic reformer and suave bureaucrat, and Party Secretary General Hu Yaobang, Deng's exuberant partner in bridge and controversial political reforms.

Aware of the damage caused by autocratic one-man rule, Deng and his colleagues are forging a collective leadership with an orderly succession of power. This framework will, they hope, endure after they depart, and ensure the continuity of modernization and democratic reforms. Deng is promoting younger professionals and technocrats into the presently aging, monolithic bureaucracy. He is urging the venerable deadwood to retire, keeping their limousines and perks but at the same time making way for the young.

Political life for the people, too, is livelier and more open than it was before, although everyone has to attend political study sessions, no one is free to criticize socialism or the Party and meaningful dissent is quickly crushed. Still, there are elections for local governments and Party committees, and the ballots are secret. Today, indeed, the hand-picked Party man does not always win.

"It makes no difference whether a cat is black or white; as long as it catches rats, it is a good cat." 79 year-old Deng Xiaoping, China's paramount leader, is more a man of action than of words. Protégé of late Premier Zhou Enlai, he has systematically steered the country away from ideological disputes onto a more pragmatic path: moderate and steady economic reconstruction at home, and a more open and independent policy abroad. He is the staunch survivor of two political purges under Mao, who once complained that when he spoke, Deng never listened. "Deng is hard of hearing," Mao grumbled, "yet at meetings he always sits as far from me as possible." Today, Deng is paving the way for all-out modernization in China, enlivening the sluggish urban industrial sector, encouraging a spirit of competition amongst the peasants, reforming government bureaucracies and forcing incompetent and aged Party officials to stew in semi-retirement. As chairman of the Party's Military Commission, Deng has ordered the veteran generals to tote the new Party line and obey orders. "As long as people say you are restoring capitalism, you have done your work well. Be afraid of nothing, neither of opposition nor of being struck down."

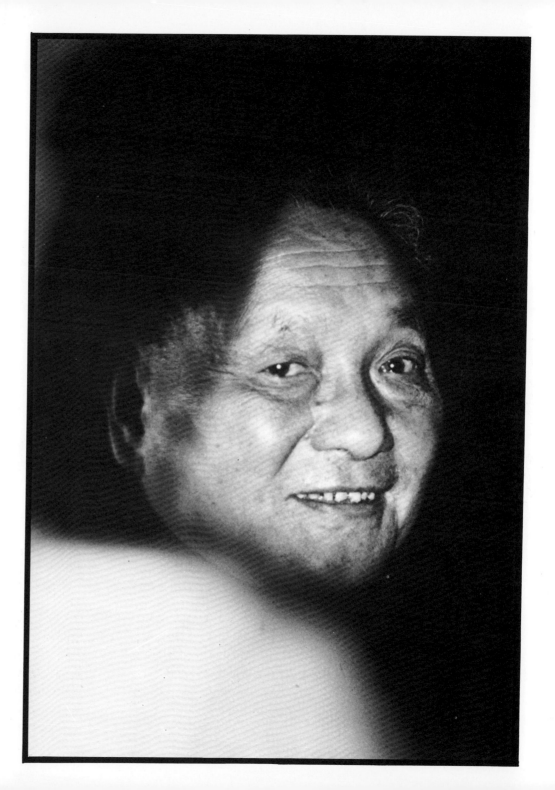

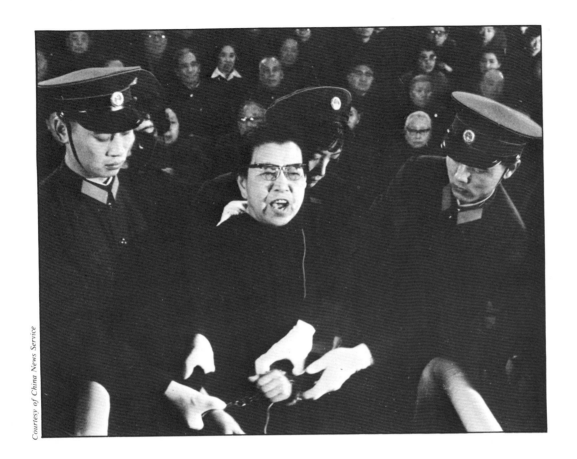

(Opposite) Four Peking youths watch the landmark trial of the Gang of Four, which lasted from Nov 1980 to Jan 1981. On the screen is Mao's widow, Jiang Qing, 69, who was arrested in Oct 1976. "You are trying to destroy me because you know you can never destroy Chairman Mao," she told the court during her trial. (Left) After being sentenced to death, Jiang Qing is dragged from the courtroom reportedly shouting, "I am lawless; what are you going to do about it?" Her sentence was commuted to life imprisonment in Jan 1983.

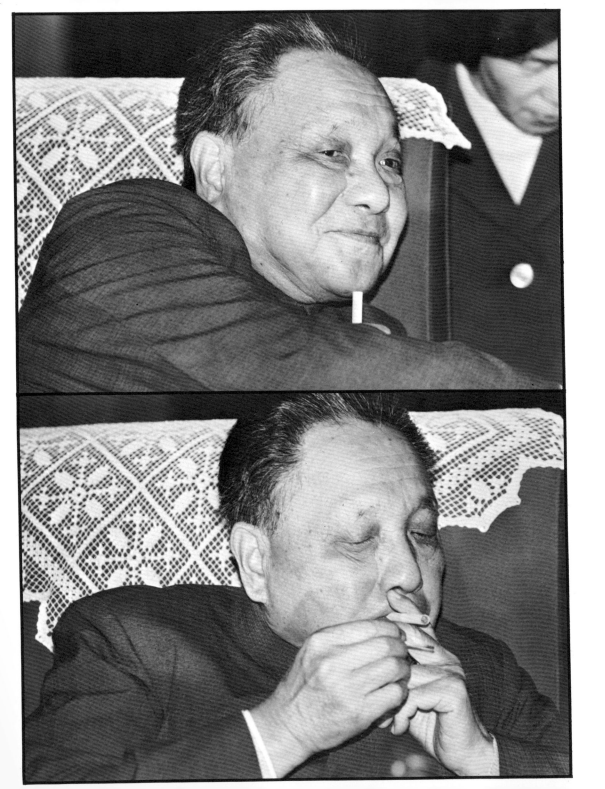

(Left) "I have two vices — smoking too much and using a spittoon. People tell me I should stop smoking, but I don't do it..." Deng Xiaoping lights a cigarette in the Fujian Room of the Great Hall of the People, 1980. (Opposite) Ma Desheng, a Chinese woodcut artist, speaks for his colleagues in front of Peking's City Hall as they demonstrate against the government for refusing them permission to exhibit avant-garde works of art.

16

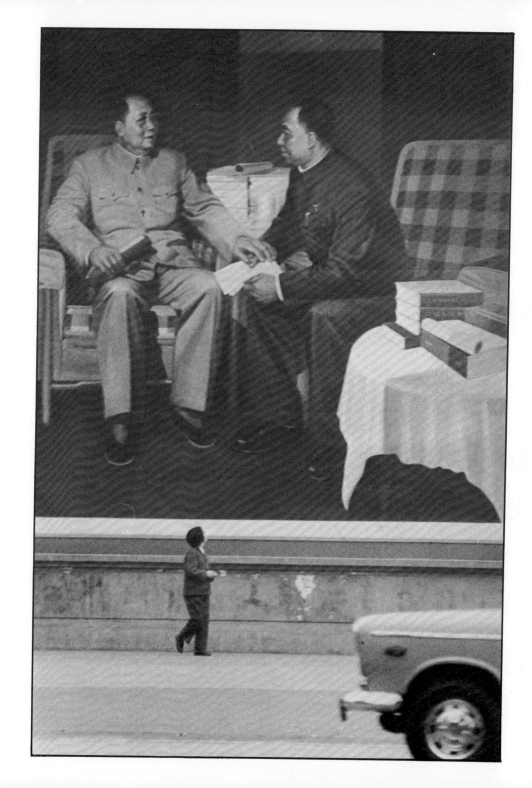

(Opposite) Giant statue of Mao attracts a young man's eye in a Shanghai Xinhua bookstore, 1980. (Right) Enormous mural in Shanghai's Bund shows Mao transferring power to his chosen successor, Hua Guofeng. "With you in charge," he was quoted as saying, "I am at ease." Once an obscure Party secretary in Hunan Province, Hua played a crucial role in overthrowing the Gang of Four in 1976. He became chairman of the Party in Oct the same year, but had to step down in 1981 for perpetuating his own personality cult. With Hua in disgrace, the Dengists have effectively ended their struggle to ease the dogmatic Maoists from top positions of power.

Peng Zhen, 81. Peking's former mayor, veteran pragmatist and powerful member of the Politburo.

(Above, left to right) Premier Zhao Ziyang, 65. A fervent supporter of Deng Xiaoping, he rose from Party secretary of Sichuan Province to premier in Sept 1980. In the rural areas of Sichuan, Zhao carried out economic reforms which allowed the peasants greater individual responsibility. Wan Li, 67. Promoted from Party secretary of Anhui Province to vice-premier in 1980, he revitalized China's vast railway system after it had nearly gone bankrupt during the Cultural Revolution. Chen Yun, 78. Member of the Standing Committee of the Politburo, he closely follows Deng Xiaoping in his enthusiasm for economic reform in China. Geng Biao, 74. Former defense minister, he visited the US in 1979 when Sino-US relations were at their best. Gu Mu, 69. Now councillor to the state, as former vice-premier he was the principal promoter of Sino-Japanese economic relations.

Peking residents vote for local district representatives to the National People's Congress, 1980.

19

(Right) A nurse dabs the face of Marshall Ye Jianying, 85, during the fifth and final session of the National People's Congress, Nov 1982. Behind Ye are two younger leaders, Premier Zhao Ziyang and Vice-Premier Wan Li. Ye stepped down as chairman of the Standing Committee of the National People's Congress in Feb 1983, but remained a member of the powerful ruling Politburo. The average age of the 25-member Politburo is 74.5. (Opposite) China after Mao. The ruling triumvirate — Zhao Ziyang, Deng Xiaoping and Hu Yaobang — stand in somber attention at a meeting marking the centenary of the death of Karl Marx, Great Hall of the People, Mar 1983.

DEMOCRACY

Students of the People's University march in Tiananmen Square in protest against the 2nd Artillery Corps of the People's Liberation Army, which had occupied portions of the campus, Oct 1979.

Veteran Korean War hero, who fought for China but still did not escape persecution during the Cultural Revolution, demands rehabilitation, Sept 1979.

Students protest against the elitist People's Liberation Army outside Zhongnanhai, the government headquarters, where many of China's leaders are in residence, Sept 1979.

Shielding the bus depot on Peking's main Chang'an Boulevard, stands an undistinguished gray brick wall. Undistinguished until for a brief exhilarating period from 1978 to 1980 it became known as "Democracy Wall." Then it was the magnet for a tiny human rights movement, a wailing wall for the wronged, the outraged and the beseeching, who covered its surface with *dazibao* (big character posters) to air their grievances in traditional style.

It was vibrant, spontaneous and risky, and every day foreign correspondents would cluster to read the latest messages. Late at night, in response to an anonymous telephone call, they would rush to read a new poster or stand by, say, the third tree on the right to await a whispered contact.

For a time, after bouncing back from his latest purge, Deng Xiaoping himself used carefully planted posters to denounce his enemies. Although he favors only limited socialist democracy, Deng encouraged the idealistic outpouring, manipulating it with utmost skill to discredit the leftists who had purged him.

Finally, however, the clamoring from Democracy Wall was too much even for Deng. Poster writers were calling for the impossible and impermissible —free love, western democracy and real elections. The demand for political freedom had become unnervingly loud and the criticism of leftists a criticism of all leaders, including Deng himself. The young idealists, unleashed for a heady moment to consolidate Deng's power, had gone too far and become an embarrassment.

Then it was over. The wall was hosed and scrubbed down at midnight, and the activists were rounded up. A new wall, soon to be dubbed "Bureaucracy Wall," where all posters were registered, replaced it for a time but was short lived. Finally the right to put up big character posters was stricken from the Constitution. Democracy Wall has returned to silence. Now, instead of protests, only billboard advertisements for heavy machinery and modernization cover its dull brick surface.

Chinese youth skates past giant statue of Mao in the Dalian Institute of Technical Management, 1981. Many such statues have been removed, but many still remain.

(Opposite) Despite the rain, concerned citizens stop to read the latest on Democracy Wall, 1979. (Above) Chinese artist Ma Desheng addresses supporters in front of Peking's municipal government building demanding the right to exhibit works which do not agree with the Party's policy on art, Oct 1979. (Right) While some study the posters on Democracy Wall, one man squats to read his *People's Daily,* the official mouthpiece of the Communist Party, 1979.

(Above) Petitioners take a meal outside their makeshift shelter, 1979. Calling themselves "refugees of China," they have traveled from the South to demand that the Party redress the wrongs they suffered at its hands during the Cultural Revolution.
(Right) Students of the People's University display a derisive poster caricature as they march in protest against the People's Liberation Army, Oct 1979.

(Right) In a Shanghai primary school, a group of young students denounces the notorious Gang of Four, 1976. (Below) One of thousands of petitioners who poured into the capital during 1980 to air their personal grievances before the government.

(Left) Pushing their way to the front of the line, citizens clamor to buy the last issue in 1979 of *Exploration,* China's most outspoken dissident magazine. Wei Jingsheng, an editor, was sentenced to 15 years imprisonment for attacking Deng and insisting that democracy in China would be necessary to successful achievement of the Four Modernizations. (Opposite, above) On the eve of the crackdown, a young man prints the transcripts of Wei Jingsheng's trial, 1979. (Opposite, below) Another dissident supporter sells the unofficial transcripts. Shortly afterwards, public security guards arrest him as well, 1979.

AFTER MAO

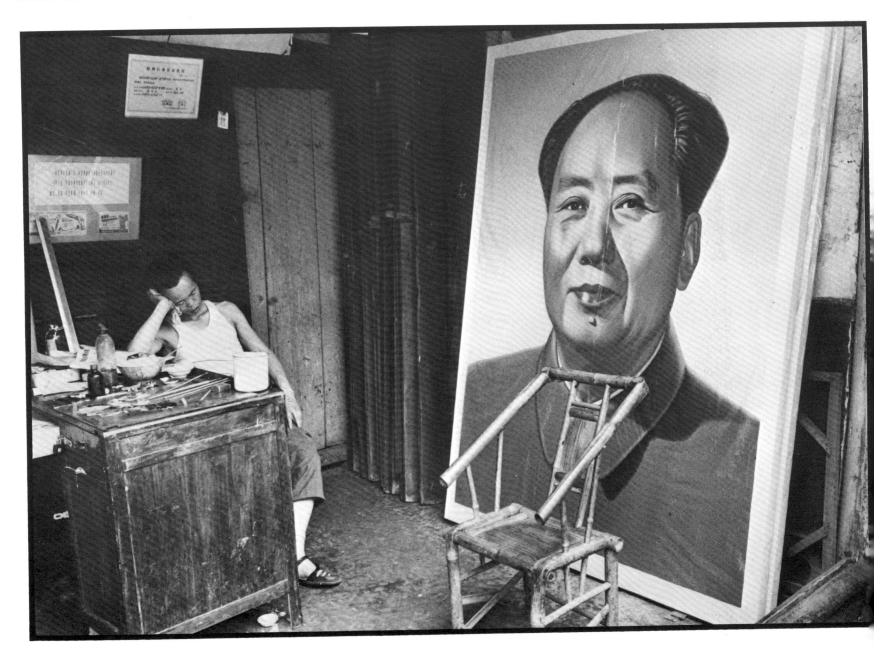

(Opposite) Artist in Chengdu, Sichuan, takes a *xiuxi* (nap) next to a large portrait of Mao Tse-tung. "Nowadays," he says, "I paint him less and less." (Above) In the studio of a Shanghai advertising agency, workers display portraits of Mao and Hua Guofeng, 1980. (Right) Peasant eats a bowl of a rice oblivious to the faded portrait of Mao sitting forgotten and half-obscured on the shelf behind him. Next to the portrait is a slogan by Hua: "Listen to Chairman Hua." Mt Emei, Sichuan, 1980.

For years Chairman Mao Tse-tung's rotund, implacable image and dogmatic, divisive ideas loomed everywhere in China, and he reigned as a modern emperor. Colossal pink or white statues of Mao towered over public squares, dwarfing his beloved masses. Monolithic portraits of Mao marred public buildings. Busts and portraits were enshrined in every home, and factories turned out glow-in-the-dark Mao buttons. Mao's "Little Red Book" was the communist Bible, and, for a time, Red Guards would halt pedestrians and order them to recite quotations.

Today China has shifted decisively from Mao to modernization, and Mao the demi-god has been toppled from his pedestal. In September 1982, the 12th Communist Party Congress repudiated Mao's ideals of class struggle and continuing revolution, and called for stability, unity and economic construction. It banned his personality cult and called for collective leadership instead of despotic one-man rule. While lip service is still paid to Mao, what remains is more form than substance. China's direction today would surely dismay the Great Helmsman as the undoing of his life's work.

The Party now says Mao was a great mortal who made great contributions in his earlier years and great mistakes later on — the Cultural Revolution was one of them. Instead of reading the Red Book, people are exhorted to "seek truth from facts." Mao's works molder in bookstores and no one buys them for pennies. In what would have been heresy a few years back, Mao is recycled into science texts, historical novels and love stories.

Workmen have pulled down Mao's lugubrious portraits from central Tiananmen Square as "unseemly and lacking in dignity." They have taken torches and burned apart his multi-story slogans. One enterprising Peking neighborhood collected Mao buttons and melted them for scrap metal.

Giant portrait of Mao is laid to rest in Peking's Museum of Communist Party History, 1981.

"Ah! Farewell Democracy Wall..." On a Sunday afternoon in 1980, a man recites poetry as he publicly mourns the loss of the dissident mouthpiece, Democracy Wall.

(Left) Peasant resting at the feet of Mao as he raises his hand in benediction of the masses. Hohhot, Inner Mongolia, 1981. (Opposite, above) Enormous propaganda billboard forms a sharp contrast to the subdued expressions of passing pedestrians. Shanghai, 1981. (Opposite, below) Young offenders march inside Tuan He Youth Reform Camp in Peking, 1982. Their crimes range from petty thieving to gang rape. The Party has called for the restoration of a just and orderly legal system in China. Unlike before, police are now told to produce arrest warrants before taking action. But the legal system is in its infancy; in Peking there are only 300 lawyers available to represent over 9 million citizens.

37

(Left) Workers take part in political study session in a Shanghai steel product factory, 1977. The ritual of endless institutionalized political studies continues in China today. (Above) Beneath portraits of Mao and Hua, which are hung throughout the nation, women workers listen to a news reading during a political study session, 1977.

(Above) Over the inevitable portrait of Mao Tse-tung hangs a large banner mourning his death, Canton, Oct 1976. (Right) Young inmates of Tuan He Youth Reform Camp brush up their studies of Marxism, 1982.

Artist in Peking's Central Fine Arts Institute puts the finishing touches to a sitting Buddha, 1982. The Institute has been commissioned to replace the statues in a Guizhou monastery smashed by Red Guards during the Cultural Revolution. Today, sculptures of Mao are less prominent, and religious statues and relics are beginning to reappear in houses of worship, rural homes and free markets.

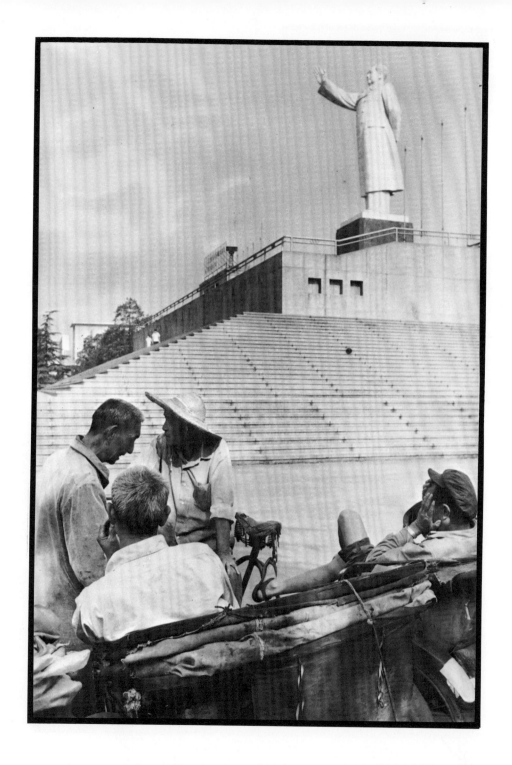

Pedicab drivers wait for customers in the square in downtown Chengdu, Sichuan. A sports stadium was planned for the site, but leftist local officials used the funds to build a towering statue of Mao instead, 1982.

(Above) At Democracy Wall, interested Peking residents gather to peruse the sketches of an "unofficial" artist who was denied access to art school and a place to exhibit his works, 1979. (Right) A member of the Communist Youth League swears allegiance to the Party, 1982.

42

(Above) One of thousands of "big character posters" bemoaning government activities is pasted up on Democracy Wall, 1979. (Right) Workers stare at a Mao portrait taken down in Tiananmen Square, 1981.

44

(Opposite) In Tuan He Youth Reform Camp, 1982, a conductor leads a group of young inmates singing, "We love socialism…" (Below) Young pioneers watch a soccer game in Shanghai, 1977. (Right) Pioneer leader salutes as his group pledges loyalty to Chinese socialism and promises to contribute to the Four Modernizations, 1981.

(Left) In Peking, a Mongolian passer-by is assailed by the amplified voices of young students as they urge the people to take part in "Ethics Month," an annual event since March 1982 to encourage politeness and cooperation in the true spirit of socialism. (Right) 1981, and yet another portrait of Mao is unceremoniously removed.

PEOPLE

Smoking break in Tiananmen Square, Peking, 1982.

In post-Mao China spirits run high — as expressed by two young adults showing off their roller skating in a Shanghai rink, 1980.

One of China's over 6 million people of Hui nationality, 1980. The Hui people, of Islamic faith, are one among many minority ethnic groups scattered throughout the nation.

Old woman in Shanghai. The average age of China's one billion people is 26. More than half the population is under 20 and only 5 percent is over 60. Although China is the world's oldest continuing civilization, its population is the world's youngest.

China's one billion people are not all preoccupied with politics, democracy and modernization. Now that the Maoist era of struggle has ended, the air is calmer, more relaxed, and the Constitution guarantees the right to leisure. People are free to play, read novels, deck themselves out in western sunglasses, buy television sets, race pigeons and vacation on the seaside.

Western dancing parties and disco were banned in 1982, and western music and styles denounced as "decadent." But dancing parties are still held in secret and even the Communist Party does not object to a sedate foxtrot. The Party's Youth League organizes "Youth Garden" dancing parties at night on pleasure boats plying the Pearl River in Canton.

But the most famous day and night spot, the hang-out fabled in the foreign press — Peking's "Peace Cafe" — is no more. It attracted too many unemployed denizens of the streets, wheeler-dealers, spoiled children of high cadres, lonely third world students and less than ladylike young ladies. So it was closed, to be reopened later under strict police supervision.

For more sedate entertainment, Chinese stroll through parks while young girls pose beside lotus ponds or shiny western cars as boyfriends snap their pictures. More affluent Chinese no longer feel satisfied with bicycles and demand motorcycles. In summer, young people crowd beaches of the Beidaihe resort northeast of Peking, drinking beer and Coca Cola. Playboys flex their muscles and women in modest bathing suits shade themselves under bonnets lest they tan and look like peasants.

Dai women on the banks of the Lancang Jiang (Mekong River) in Yunnan Province, 1980. One of China's minority nationalities, the Dai people are scattered over the border areas of Yunnan and Burma.

Smart couple in western suits secure a future reminder of May Day, 1982.

(Above) In freezing sub-zero temperatures, this couple carries a child wrapped in heavy quilts across the frozen Songhua River in Harbin, a city once referred to as "Moscow of the East," 1981. (Below) Attractive young woman strikes a pose in Beidaihe, Gulf of Bohai — a seaside resort once reserved exclusively for elite government officials, diplomats, literati, movie stars and their offspring, 1982.

(Above) Young couple proudly displays a Sanyo cassette tape recorder playing popular love songs — which the authorities would in their more rhetorical moments damn as ''yellow pornographic music,'' Orange Island outside Changsha, Hunan, 1981. (Below) Young peasant girl harvests rice in Shaoshan, the birthplace of Mao Tse-tung. During the Cultural Revolution, peasants in the area planted rice in rows that said, ''Long Live Liu Shaoqi,'' a late president of China, already persecuted at the time for daring to disagree with Mao's radical economic policies.

(Left) An exuberant crowd is on the brink of drenching a public security guard during the annual Water Splashing Festival in Xishuangbanna, Yunnan, 1980. The festival forms part of the traditional Dai celebration of the Solar New Year. (Below) Complementing the ceremony, Dai traditional dancers wearing Chinese Army caps carouse in a village in Jinghong, Yunnan, 1980.

Chinese peasants of Li Yan Commune dance on stilts to hail the Lunar New Year in Peking, 1980. Nearly all such traditional customs were spurned during the chaotic decade of 1966-76.

(Above, left) Youths share a moment of laughter at the chess board in Shanghai's Fuxing Park, 1978. (Below, left) The Chinese paper chase: high school students study under the lights in Tiananmen Square, 1981. Gone are the days when students could hand in blank papers at examinations and declare themselves heroes of the anti-intellectual movement. Formal university entrance examinations resumed in 1977. (Opposite) Relaxing in front of Peking's railway station, 1981.

(Left) Retired men enjoy the time-honored tradition of tea drinking at the Yu Yuan Tea House in the old quarter of Shanghai, 1979. Here unemployed educated youths are encouraged to sell peanuts, watermelon seeds and cigarettes. (Opposite) China's punks. Three boys at Simao, Yunnan province, 1980.

(Opposite) In Mao's China, keeping songbirds or goldfish as pets was cast as a sign of bourgeois decadence. Now, as aesthetic appreciation makes its comeback, an old man loads his side-car with once forgotten cages of birds. Longtan Park, Peking, 1982.

(Above) Posing together for a beach portrait in Beidaihe resort, 1982. Beidaihe, with its white beaches and Mediterranean ambiance, was built many years ago for foreign diplomats - no Chinese allowed. Here, from his seaside bunker, former Minister of Defense Lin Biao plotted the abortive coup d'état which was to land him in a plane crash in Outer Mongolia in 1971. Today the town evokes more indolence than intrigue, although the Communist Party still holds meetings here from time to time. (Right) Young man in chic designer sunglasses poses for a picture in Beidaihe resort where the affluent sons and daughters of army generals are often to be seen cruising down the Beach Road in their private foreign cars — a dramatic sign of class distinction in China's proletarian society.

(Above) Peace Cafe, 1979. Once it was the liveliest nightspot in Peking, where young people would gather to smoke expensive foreign cigarettes, drink Chinese champagne soda and win the admiration of lonely third world students. After a few fleeting months it was closed down. Some young women were dragged away by public security guards and charged with prostitution. (Left) Shanghai Department Store, the largest in the country, 1978.

(Above) In 1981, Coca Cola opened its first plant in Peking. Though some Chinese say that Coke tastes like "medicine," the plant now produces 48 million bottles a year. "The potential here is tremendous," said Coke Chairman Roberto Goizueta, who flew in to Peking for the official opening ceremony. (Below) "It tastes so-so..." said one young man spotted drinking Coke in the Imperial Palace, 1981.

(Right) Cyclists ride the new highway in the Jianguomenwai district of Peking. According to a 1981 government survey, there are 95 million bicycles in China — one for every ten people. (Opposite, above) Cruising down Chang'an Boulevard, neatly turned-out motorcyclists greet fellow motorists, 1982. The woman wears a thin transparent scarf over her head to protect herself from the sand-laden winds which blow from Siberia across the North China Plain in winter. (Opposite, below) Solitary mule-ride through the desolate town of Siziwan, Inner Mongolia, 1980. Along this vast border area, and in many of the inland provinces, mules are still a major source of transportation.

(Opposite) Generations apart in Yungming Yuan Park near the Summer Palace, 1982. With his "Hell's Angel" image, a young man leans on his shiny imported motorcycle while an old woman sits astride a marble turtle doing her needlework. (Above) Chinese macho flexes his muscles, Beidaihe resort, 1982. (Right) Chinese sit in the hard seats of the Lanzhou-Urumqi train, fondly referred to by the peasants as the "Iron Rooster," 1982. Despite the egalitarian nature of their society, the Chinese still have three classes on their trains. Senior cadres naturally ride in the first class "soft sleeper" where passengers are able to order more than just a bowl of noodles for their meals.

Outside her home in Hunan, the world's tallest woman, Zheng Qinlian (2.4 m), hobbles along supported by her mother and aunt. She died at the age of 16 weighing 147 kg (324 pounds).

(Above) Pu Jie, the 76 year-old brother of the last Manchu Emperor, Pu Yi, strikes a pose in his former residence, the Imperial Palace. "Once upon a time," he says serenely, "I used to be up there. I am the last Manchu." (Left) Sun Yaoting, 80, one of the three remaining eunuchs living in Peking. Sun entered the Palace in 1916 during the last days of the Ching Dynasty, and earned 20 taels of silver a month as the chosen eunuch of the fickle teen-aged Empress Wang Rong. Now Sun lives quietly in Drum Tower Street, tending flowers and goldfish in the elegant courtyard of a former monastery.

A polaroid snapshot evokes a smile aboard the train from Shanghai to Peking, 1980.

Old women with bound feet laugh at their distorted reflections Peking's Ritan Park, 1979.

Tibetan Lama priest strokes his goatee beard before the legendary Potala Palace in Lhasa, 1982. In an effort to woo the Dalai Lama back to Tibet from his exile in India, the government has embarked on a policy of "Tibetanization." Since 1981, 11,000 ethnic Han have been sent back home to allow the Tibetan cadres to administer local affairs in their medieval "roof of the world."

MODERNIZATION

Two generations of travel on a highway in Shenzhen, 1981. Since 1979, the central government has created four special economic trade zones, including Shenzhen, in an effort to attract foreign investments — a significant move in its decision to "open up the country to the outside world." The new policy forms a direct contrast with previous decades of self-imposed isolation in China.

Listening to AT&T cartoon character telephones, Chinese are fascinated by American technology at a US exhibition in Peking, 1981. China still regards foreign technology with some circumspection. Exhibits are common, but Chinese authorities remain cautious as to what and how much to import to promote modernization.

China can launch satellites and create nuclear weapons, but only about 25 percent of its people can read and write, and the world's most populous country has not moved far beyond the age of the abacus and the water buffalo. Man is still the dominant draft animal.

When China's undisputed leader and reformer, Deng Xiaoping, went to the United States in late 1978, China's privileged television viewers saw the Peachtree Center in Atlanta, Georgia. Many said they were overwhelmed and disillusioned by their own backwardness, wondering if what was once a great civilization could ever be so again.

In December the same year, the Communist Party Central Committee broke with the Maoist legacy of politics-in-command and continuing class struggle. In its place it proclaimed a course of economic reform, dubbed the ''Four Modernizations,'' in which China would open to the west and import foreign technology. The policy is based on modernizing industry (with the shift decisively toward light industry and consumer goods), agriculture, defense, science and technology.

But China, stunted as it is by political strife, and shackled by feudalism, faces an excruciating task. Mao and his radicals persecuted intellectuals and scientists, burned books, smashed laboratories and destroyed the educational system. Workers, peasants and soldiers were considered superior to intellectuals. Brawn, not books, was needed for modernization.

Today China has 10,000 students and scholars in the US alone on a mission to modernize. Yet on the outskirts of cities, peasants still scrape up manure from the road for fertilizer, and nightsoil remains a national asset. Under the neon lights of the new Jianguo (build the nation) Hotel in Peking, old men in mule carts slumber as their beasts clop home to the suburbs. Ask a man what he thinks of modernization as he stands behind his water buffalo in his ancestral rice paddies, and he is likely to say, "I never thought about it."

(Left) Construction workers put in time on the Baoshan steel plant, which will cost 5 billion US dollars to build using Japanese and West German technology, 1982. Approximately 1.5 billion US dollars worth of equipment was provided for the project by Japanese companies. (Center) On Peking's Changping Road, an old man sweeps up horse excrement for fertilizer, 1980.
(Right) Reaching for the phone, in a control room of the "East is Red" Oil Refinery on the outskirts of Peking, 1980. In 1982, China produced 102 million tons of crude oil on its own, but invited major western oil companies to bid for drilling rights in its offshore waters.

Advertising billboard for Gold-Fish pencils disrupts the serene vista of the Forbidden City and nearby Beihai Park, 1981. Once, advertising was denounced as an exploitative tool used only by bourgeois capitalists. Now state corporations rely on advertising to sell everything from cosmetics to tractors.

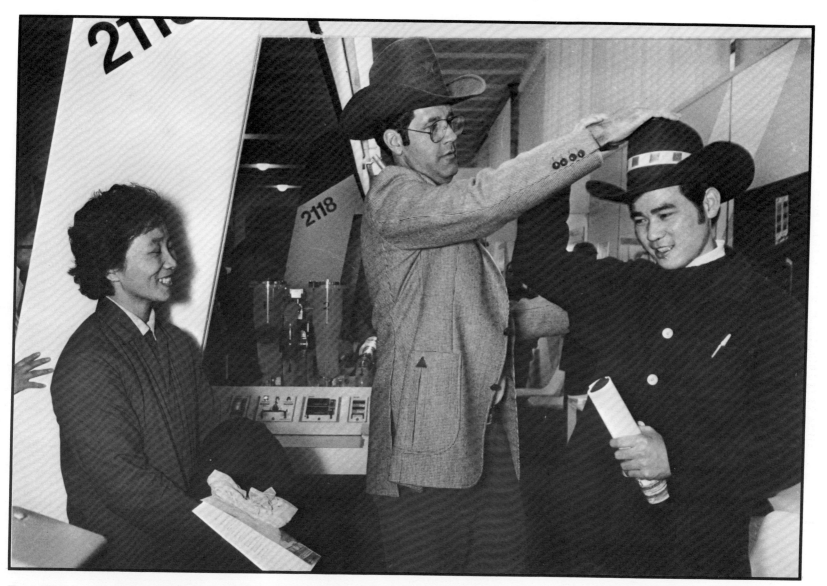

Fred Ward, a bullish Texan oil explorer, helps a Chinese viewer with a cowboy hat at the US National Economic and Trade Exhibition, Nov 1980. During the exhibition, tons of sophisticated US equipment were put on display. The selective introduction of foreign technology is encouraged, but China still maintains a policy of self-reliance.

Still life at the Yanshan Petroleum Refinery in Peking, 1980.

(Left) Shanghai peasant with Chinese-made hand-held tractor in a rice field in Ma Lu Commune, 1978. In most parts of China, arable lands are not flat enough for the use of heavier machines. (Below) Village boys tend a water buffalo in Yu Lu Commune, 1981. Here peasants are beginning to adopt the production responsibility system whereby, having met the government quota, they are allowed to sell any extra produce in local free markets. Especially in the more conservative provinces such as Hunan, Party commune cadres were reluctant to adopt the new system because it implied that they themselves would have to do manual labor. They far preferred to remain in administrative positions earning "work points" for doing nothing, critics said.

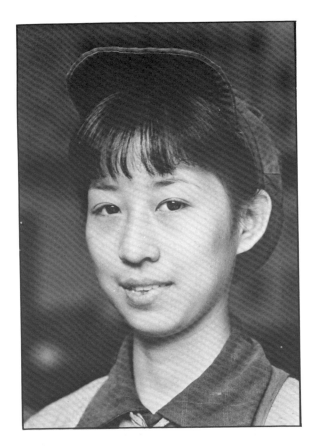

(Right) 16 year-old coalminer near Datong, Shanxi Province, 1982. (Above) Shanghai woman worker in a steel pipe factory, 1977.

(Below) Whipping up a bucket of yak milk on top of a tractor in Lhasa, 1982. This Tibetan peasant lives with his family in the tent behind him. (Left to right) A smiling coalminer in Datong, and a government bureaucrat in Peking, 1982.

Shantou (formerly Swatow) fishermen hoe the sand for land reclamation; behind them is a foreign cargo ship, 1981. The village was first transformed into a bustling port when Britain forced China to open five coastal cities to trade after the Opium Wars. Now Shantou is one of the nation's four special economic trade zones.

Oct 1976. Unruffled by the news announcing the death of Mao, a worker in Canton demonstrates *wushu* **— one of the Chinese martial arts — to his friends in People's Square.**

(Below) Electronic equipment assembly line in a joint venture factory in Shenzhen, 1981. Here workers earn triple the salary of those in state-operated enterprises where more work is not yet rewarded with higher pay. (Right) A new television set is strapped to a Suzuki mo-ped outside Peking's Friendship store — open only to foreigners and overseas Chinese, 1980. Public security officers generally guard the doors, and all but an enterprising few with the right connections are prevented from stepping in. (Opposite) The Shanghai, China's copy of the 1950's Mercedes Benz, takes shape in a Shanghai car factory with the help of a woman worker. This model sells for 20,000 yuan (10,000 US dollars).

(Right) Near the rice paddies of Guilin, Guangxi Autonomous Region, a young peasant girl sells miniature trees and rockeries. Countless karst hills and a lush green river valley make Guilin the most scenic spot in China. (Opposite) Peasants at Evergreen Commune toss cabbages, the only vegetable available to the northern Chinese in winter, onto a slow-moving truck, 1980. Later, the cabbages will be bought in bulk and piled for storage in courtyards or on terraces. Today the commune system is steadily being abandoned for more efficient methods designed to raise productivity. The peasants themselves are all too eager to smash the socialist "Iron Rice Bowl."

Western television shows, such as "The Man from Atlantis," have become all-time hits in China. The country now has 7 million TV sets — one for every 140 people. Here, on Shanghai's Nanjing Road, an advertisement for Sony dramatically transforms the city landscape. (Above) Listening through earphones to an audio-visual demonstration at a US national exhibition of technology and equipment, 1982.

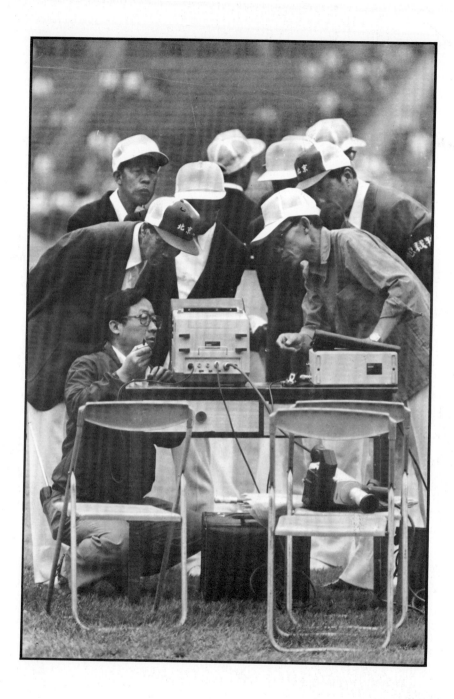

(Right) Chinese sports officials study a time-keeping instrument during a national track and field competition in the Peking Workers' Stadium. With the government to back them, Chinese athletes have come into their own in recent years. China took 61 gold medals in the 1982 Asian Games in New Delhi, eclipsing Japan for the first time in history. "We are no longer the sick man of Asia," the sports news proclaimed.

(Right) Watching for customers in a Peking free market — where Chinese can now shop if they have the money. Today, the economy at grass-root level is more active than in the past when it was stifled by ultra-leftist policies. But China too is feeling the pinch of the inflation which has plagued other nations. Although the government puts inflation at about 3 percent, foreign analysts believe it is probably closer to 10 percent. (Opposite) Dongdan Market, Peking, 1979. Chinese consumers have complained repeatedly of bad service at state-owned stores. In response, the government launched the campaign of the "Five Stresses and Four Beauties": Decorum, courtesy, public health, discipline and morals are to be stressed, and the mind, language, behavior and environment are to be beautified.

Primary school kids give each other haircuts in a classroom barber shop in Shanghai, 1977. During the Cultural Revolution, "little rebels" cursed and threw things at their teachers. In post-Mao China, teachers are shown the respect they deserve.

94

Clement Chen, an expatriate Chinese-American from Palo Alto, California, has opened China's first deluxe class hotel, the Jianguo, in cooperation with the Peking branch of the China International Travel Service. The 25 million US dollar, 445-room hotel is a capitalist island in a proletarian sea — "I'm making a revolution," said Chen, "and I'll show them what service is all about."

Mitsubishi leaves its mark on Shanghai's Nanjing Road. China's busiest boulevard, it attracts 150,000 out-of-towners a year to the city once known as "Paris of the East."

Much of China's northern frontier is bare, with nothing to mark the landscape save miles and miles of power poles, a unique sign of change in these remote border areas. Here, in the desolate town of Siziwan, Inner Mongolia, an army truck looms on the horizon. It is a bleak reminder of the "Northern Polar Bear" — the 50 divisions of Soviet troops stationed just across the border.

THE ARMY

PLA 6th Armored Division troop in Peking, 1980.

The 4.23 million-strong People's Liberation Army has been called a "state within a state." It remains a formidable political force with which every government and Party leader must reckon.

Although deprived of rank insignia during the egalitarian mania of the Cultural Revolution, Army officers still receive homage, privileges, housing and limousines that surpass those of mere government officials. The PLA is an insulated, self-sufficient world where soldiers grow their own food, run their own factories and help peasants harvest grain, build roads and construct dams.

The Army, too, is the last bastion of Maoism and statues of Mao raise their hands in eerie benediction over many an Army unit. Its warriors, mostly peasants, were weaned on Mao's gospel of "People's War" — the invincible human wave — and on his unquestioned quotations.

But this army of communist warlords, and peasants too, must modernize in post-Mao China. No matter how great the human factor nor how brave the human heart, people's war cannot win over nuclear weapons, and the guerrilla era has ended. Now the PLA is reducing its size, demanding education, technical training and better weapons to upgrade its solid but outdated arsenal. It is replacing rote study of Mao's doctrines with professional education and conducting military exercises using modern tactics.

China's performance during its December 1978 invasion of Vietnam was less than magnificent, and its military forces need to be strengthened. But the shift away from ideology within the Army, and the trend outside it toward making more money is leaving many foot soldiers uneasy and reluctant to stay. While soldiering still is considered honorable, it only pays 6 to 36 yuan a month (3 US dollars for a private to 18 US dollars for a sergeant).

Impoverished heroes have trouble winning brides. Many young men would rather stay down on the farm where, helped by today's new economic policies, they can become rich peasants instead.

Soldier of the People's Liberation Army in Peking Airport, 1979.

99

(Opposite) Senior Army officials and leading Party cadres study documents at meeting marking the centenary of Karl Marx' death, Great Hall of the People, Mar 1983. At the meeting, Party leader Hu Yaobang stressed that China is advancing Marxism, "giving up old forms divorced from reality." (Left) PLA soldier stands by a Chinese-made tank before inspection by US Secretary of Defense Harold Brown, who visited the 6th Armored Division of the PLA in Jan 1980 when Sino-US relations were at their best. Today, both nations have grown suspicious of each other, and Peking has consistently referred to US arms sales to the Nationalists in Taiwan as the "dark cloud over the horizon."

Inside the ornate Great Hall of People, senior commanders of the PLA sit chatting quietly, 1980.
Under the chairmanship of Deng Xiaoping, the Military Commission persuaded these old generals to step aside for the younger officers who are more in tune with modern warfare tactics, and accept graciously the posts of advisers. Although some Red Army veterans agreed to relinquish their posts, many still refuse to step down.

102

Smiling PLA airport guard sits beneath a civilian CAAC An-24 passenger plane at Simao Airport, Yunnan Province.

Chinese aerospace workers closely follow a briefing on British Harrier-C jump jets at the British Aerospace Exhibition in Shanghai, 1980. China is known to be interested in buying some of these versatile jet fighters which are capable of vertical take-off. But while the PLA is anxious to modernize its aging fleet of fighter planes, it has been forced to accept cuts in China's defense spending, and many such sensitive purchases have been put on ice.

China's upgraded Mig-19 interceptors scramble from the runway of the military airport of Yangcun where the 31st Division of the Chinese Airforce is based, 1980. The Chinese-made version of the Soviet Mig-19 is China's equivalent to the US F-6.

(Above) A platoon leader of the 587th Regiment of the 196th Division of the PLA inspects his troops during a drill session at the base in Yangcun near Tianjin, 1982. (Right) PLA soldier directs traffic at the headquarters of the 196th Division, while behind him looms the familiar statue of Mao, 1982. Many soldiers and officers are unhappy with life after demobilization, for they are no longer assigned the privileged jobs and positions guaranteed them before the era of economic reform. (Opposite, above and below) Target shooting practice, 1982. The Army, which sought to teach the Vietnamese "a lesson" in 1979, was taught an important one instead. After its less than admirable performance, the PLA later admitted that many of its officers were too old for combat. And that the Vietnamese, having fought the Americans for many years, had proved to be a formidable foe.

(Opposite) Young woman militia member is coached during shooting practice in Peking, 1980. In virtually all Chinese organizations, and especially in factories, every able-bodied man and woman is duty-bound to join the militia, which is sometimes called in to assist police patrols. In times of war, militia members are trained to fight alongside regular PLA forces.

(Above) Naval Honor Guards march in Tiananmen Square before inspection by a visiting head of state, 1982. The PLA Navy, with its aging fleet, remains essentially a defensive force guarding China's long coastline. (Left) Soldiers march with bayonet-armed rifles in Peking, 1982. Officially, the PLA claims that the concept of fighting a "People's War" is still valid. But in 1982 the Army staged a series of modern warfare exercises with simulated attacks from both land and air. The largest maneuver was held in Zhangjiakou in May 1982, while a month later tactical nuclear weapons were used in an exercise in Ningxia.

(Left) Operating a noodle-making machine in an Army kitchen base, 1982. Privates, who earn about 2 to 4 US dollars a month in stipend, have become harder to recruit as most peasant youths now prefer to stay in the countryside and engage in the more profitable side-line productions sanctioned by China's new economic policies. (Opposite) Along the moated wall of the Forbidden City, factory worker militia members take aim during a practice exercise. As the men learn to shoot, two women work quietly on their embroidery.

(Left) **PLA soldier guards the bridge across the Yangtze River as a cyclist rides by. Between them stands an enormous stone sculpture of the ''heroic soldier, worker and peasant,'' Nanjing, 1981. In Mao's China, political leaders tried to forget that intellectuals also existed. (Opposite) Three soldiers brandish the red flag of China during a ceremony in 1982. The Army is told to support the central government's policies, to be disciplined and to follow orders — come what may. It remains the last bastion of Maoist ideology.**

LOVE & BEAUTY

Beauty, once repressed, reviled and buried beneath baggy clothes, is rebounding to its place of honor in China. In what for years was a sere and somber society, the renaissance and renewed appreciation of beauty can now be seen in a touch of lipstick, the swirl of a skirt, the tending of a flower or the care of a songbird.

During the Cultural Revolution, women were reprimanded for their vanity, and some even bound their breasts beneath bland Maoist shrouds. But today beauty, color, individuality, even sexuality are back with a force that will be difficult to stem. Witness the pastel scarves, innocent summer dresses, fitted trousers and even painted nails.

Glamorous covergirls now sell everything from cashmere sweaters to heavy machinery. On Sundays women promenade in parks, peeking out from under parasols, striking sexy poses for their shutterbug boyfriends. Some even undergo plastic surgery to widen their eyes.

Likewise love, once considered bourgeois and selfish, abounds reassuringly — to the distress of puritanical social planners. Young people stroll frankly arm-in-arm. They crowd benches along Shanghai's Bund and rustle the bushes at night. In one thronged park, sly, entrepreneurial kids charge lovers one yuan (50 US cents) for space on a crowded bench. Love is the constant theme of songs, books, films and plays. Newspapers give advice to the lovelorn and urge the jilted not to seek revenge, while the Communist Party plays cupid, setting up matchmaking centers all over the country.

In China, however, love is for keeps and for marriage, and sex for the unmarried is supposed to be taboo. Marriage itself is forbidden until men are 22 and women are 20. In the official version, married couples are instructed to be chaste, make love rarely, then go straight to sleep and conserve their energy for socialism.

Shanghai, 1978. There is little privacy in China and lovers are often forced to hold their romantic rendezvous in the parks.

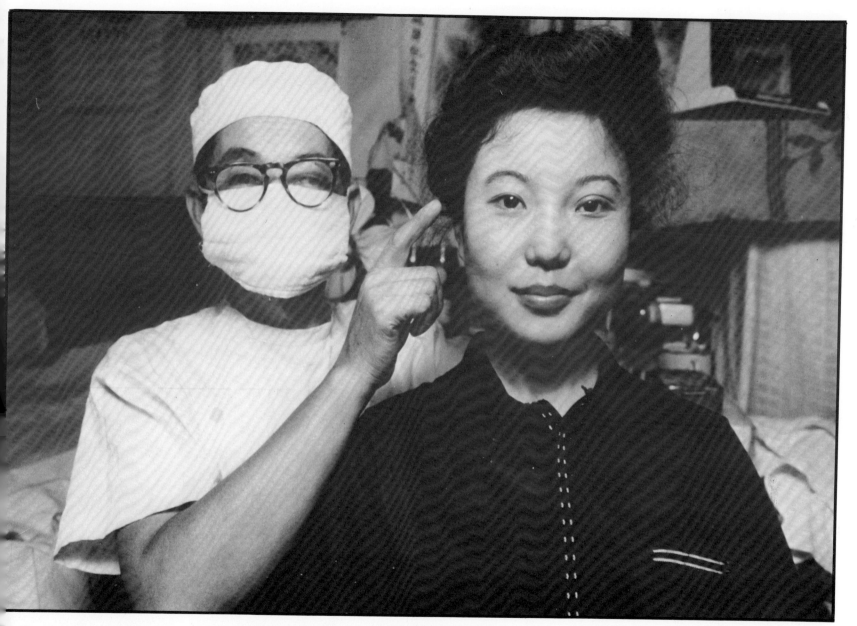

Dr Fu Nongyu points to the eyes of a patient who has undergone plastic surgery to give herself the "double eyelids" common to Western features. He is the only private plastic surgeon in Peking who performs "eye jobs," operating on one eye only at a time so that the patient is still able to cycle home. The business of beauty is booming in Peking.

Fashion-conscious women subject themselves to the permanent wave in a Peking hair salon, 1981.

(Above) Proud young hair stylist, tools in hand, lures the girls in Canton to his salon with a poster of an elegant western model. He works in the Dong Fang Hotel, which is open only to overseas Chinese and foreigners, but confesses to earning more money in his spare time styling the hair of girls who are not allowed to enter the hotel. (Below) Zhang Yu, who was China's top actress in 1980, earns 21 US dollars a month and, like everyone else, rides to and from work every day on a bicycle.

So near and yet so far. An old man contemplates a young couple on a park bench in Shanghai, 1978. Despite China's recent exposure to modern western influences, many young people confess that their parents still arrange marriages for them.

Two young Dai women squat while a friend cools himself with a paper fan in Xishuangbanna, 1980. China is a unified multi-national country with the Han nationality comprising approximately 94 percent of the total population, and 56 minority nationalities making up the other 6 percent. Two-thirds of the minority groups are distributed over the province of Yunnan, the home of 839,797 Dai people according to the 1982 census.

(Left) Foxtrotting aboard a cruise down Pearl River in Canton, 1982. The cruise organized by the local Youth League, a proceeds from the tickets usually are ab sorbed by factories where League memb work. (Below) Two couples express dif ferent moods in Shanghai's Fuxing Park 1978. Behind them a large red and whit banner reads, "Learn from Daqing" — China's largest oilfield, used as a model campaigns to encourage self-reliant in dustrial development. (Opposite) Flaunt the latest in fashion at the marble wall Peking's Beihai Park, 1981.

(Left) Candid shot in Beidaihe, Gulf of Bohai, 1982. (Below) Middle-aged couple strolls in Tiananmen Square, the woman's head veiled by a thin transparent scarf to protect her eyes and hair from the fierce sandstorms which hit Peking around March every year, 1982. (Opposite) Family mourns the death of a dear one in a Shanghai funeral parlor, 1977. During the Cultural Revolution, such acts were frowned upon as manifestations of feudalism. But today people are left more to themselves to follow their own beliefs.

Panda Wei Wei, whose stage trick is to eat candies with a knife and fork, receives a kiss from his trainer, Luo Xinqi, of the Shanghai Acrobatic Troupe. Like most of the Chinese people, Wei Wei has grown tired of the socialist "Iron Rice Bowl." Thus he and the Troupe have decided to adopt the new economic responsiblity system. This way, the more Wei Wei performs, the more candies he gets to eat.

Close friends cherish a moment of intimacy in Moon Altar Park, the site of the ill-fated attempt to create a second Democracy Wall once the original had been hosed and scrubbed down by the authorities, 1981.

Fondling in the shadows near Peking's zoo, 1981.

(Left) Members of China's new ''with it'' generation hang out near Peking's Beihai Park, 1981. The Party has expressed concern over a ''moral crisis'' amongst today's Chinese youth, and their increasing lack of confidence in communism. A recent opinion poll at Shanghai's prestigious Fudan University showed that 67 percent of the students did not believe in communism. (Below) Adorned with a new pair of sunglasses, a woman studies her reflection in the mirror while others wait anxiously at the sales counter during a Peking products exhibition in 1981.

Newlyweds in western dress pose for a portrait in Peking's Capitol Studio, 1980. To save money, this woman rented only the top half of a white wedding gown.

"Smile!" In full western regalia, another couple follows the photographer's cue, 1982.

Zhang Bin, 29, and his wife Su Bei, 24, show their wedding portrait on the train between Peking and Harbin, 1982. Son of an arms factory Party secretary and consequent member of the privileged class, Zhang can afford to take his bride on honeymoon and ride in the ''soft sleeper'' section of the train.

Shanghai youths form a caravan carrying a bridegroom's gifts — quilted bedding, chest, lacquered chamber- pot and other daily necessities — to the suburban home of the bride, 1980.

(Above) Midst enthusiastic applause, a young woman sings of socialist love at a mass wedding ceremony in the Workers' Cultural Palace, Peking, 1980. (Right) Brides and bridegrooms cluster for a mass wedding, 1980. The marriages are blessed by Peking officials who discourage lavish occasions, urging young people to opt for the more frugal mass wedding (costing one yuan — 50 US cents — per couple).

Lighting up in Xijiao Park, Shanghai, 1976.

1981. This Nanjing Protestant church was completely destroyed by Red Guards during the Cultural Revolution. Its walls still bear the traces of faded Party slogans: Long Live the Chinese Communist Party, Long Live Chairman Mao. Many churches were occupied and used as warehouses in the catastrophic decade of 1966-76.

During the Cultural Revolution temples were shattered, lamaseries razed, mosques ruined, churches smashed and holy objects desecrated. Public worship was banned as feudal superstition. Priests and monks were ridiculed, paraded through the streets and forced to do manual labor.

But the religious spirit was not extinguished. Religion has been resurrected in post-Mao China by leaders who realized they were alienating both the masses and deeply religious ethnic minorities in strategic border regions. The new Constitution guarantees the right to religious freedom, and the right to propagate atheism.

Some young believers say they would never admit their religious convictions. Yet, with a passion that has unsettled the authorities, the Chinese people have poured back into their temples, mosques and churches. Houses of worship, many defiled with political slogans and turned into warehouses and stables, are now being hastily, often gaudily restored.

Although the loss of religious art at the hands of rampaging Red Guards remains incalculable, statues are being replaced. Seminaries and training schools for monks have reopened, shrines again dot the countryside and peasants stream to leave offerings of food and burn incense. Crucifixes, Buddhas and charms to ward off the "evil eye" are on sale, and private tombstone markers are back on the market, requiring payment of a license fee and tax to the state.

The outpouring of religious sentiment is so intense, even among the young, that authorities have begun to remind the people that China is an atheist country. They warn errant Party members that communists may not believe in any god. Those who are superstitious or religious are re-educated or expelled. Nevertheless, millions of pilgrims, old and young, hobbling and healthy, still make their way to the misted heights and gutted shrines of China's sacred mountains.

(Right, above) In Peking's Church of the Immaculate Conception, young and middle-aged Catholics pray on Sunday, 1980. (Right, below) Devout Tibetans prostrate themselves in front of the Johkang temple in the old quarter of the city of Lhasa, 1982. (Left, above) Peking Catholics pray at a Sunday church service. There are 3 million Chinese Catholics and 700,000 Protestants, many of whom were persecuted during past decades for their religious beliefs. Today, some Catholics still choose to remain faithful to the Pope and the Vatican despite China's refusal to establish relations until the severing of Vatican ties with Taiwan. (Left, below) Chinese Moslems at a service in Peking's Dongsi Mosque, 1980. There are 7 million Islamic believers nationwide, many of whom were forced to go against their faith by eating pork during the Cultural Revolution.

135

(Above) Young Catholic follows the ritual of daily morning worship, 1982. (Opposite, left) Catholic priest leads the choir on Easter Sunday in Peking's Church of the Immaculate Conception, 1982. In the past, many priests were forced to leave their churches to do manual labor in the countryside. Now religious souvenirs are sold outside the churches on Sundays, and in 1982, China printed one million copies of the Bible. Yet despite the new religious freedom, Catholics are warned to beware of foreign influences within the Church. (Opposite, right) Elderly Catholic women, who survived China's religious Dark Age, pray at a service in Peking, 1979. Some "loyalist" Catholics still refuse to enter government-sanctioned churches which have not been blessed by the Vatican.

Confession before a Catholic priest in the Church of the Immaculate Conception, 1979. Mass in China is still conducted in Latin.

Dai women light candles and present offerings at a Buddhist temple in Jinghong, 1980. Like other religions in China, Buddhism is going through a process of revitalization. And ancient superstitious beliefs, for which many were persecuted and killed in past decades, are once again raising their heads in the countryside.

(Right) Tibetan Lama priest meditates near a tarnished mural in Sera Monastery, 1982. Over the past two years, the Chinese government has spent 3 million yuan (1.5 million US dollars) to refurbish Lamaist temples and monasteries, an action designed as much to attract tourists as to appease the Tibetans. (Opposite, below) Young Tibetan holds up a precious button portraying the god-king, Dalai Lama, 1982. "I want him to return," he says. China has adopted significant measures to raise the standard of living of its impoverished Tibetan Society. Since 1952, 5,073 million yuan (2,500 million US dollars) has been poured into capital construction in Tibet. Today, 70 percent of the population is still illiterate. (Opposite, above) Aging pilgrims pray at dawn on the Golden Summit of Mt Emei, 1980. They plead for prosperity, good crops and fat pigs. Peasant women too old and frail to make the pilgrimage alone are carried to the Summit on the backs of young men who charge 40 fen (20 US cents) a kilometer.

ARTS & INTELLECTUAL

Chairman Mao ordained that art should serve politics, prompting China to surrender a barrage of tedious, artless propaganda — posters of ecstatic steel workers, ditties about happy nightsoil haulers and poems like, "The Communist Party is our Sunshine."

"The more you know," said Chairman Mao, "the more foolish you become." Books were burned or banned. Paintings and music with enduring human themes and ancient honorable motifs were banned too. Only revolutionary art was permitted. Peking Opera became the sterile tool of Mao's wife, Jiang Qing, who sanctioned no more than eight revolutionary sample plays.

Today the arts have been somewhat resuscitated, and artists told to serve the people and socialism — a formula permitting slightly more creativity. Still, freedom to challenge convention has not yet been given by the tiers of cultural arbiters, and the value of unique, individual perception has not been acknowledged.

Abstract art may not be hung in public. It invites varied interpretation, and in the Chinese system, where fundamental precepts must not be questioned, only one interpretation is allowed. In a Peking exhibition in September 1981, China asked the Boston Museum to take down 13 abstracts by prestigious painters such as Jackson Pollock. The museum and US Embassy refused, the paintings stayed, and crowds were pleasantly bewildered but seemingly unharmed.

Artists may now paint nudes and abstracts in their studios without the fear that they will be denounced for decadence and banished to a cowshed, but China is still prudish about nudes. An exquisite mural in Peking Airport has been boarded up because it shows a stylized female nude at an ethnic water splashing festival. A film that satirized Mao worship and questioned the wisdom of the Communist Party was banned without ever being shown in public. And the screenwriter Bai Hua was once forced to make a public self-criticism. Such are the realities of China's new, "free" art world.

(Opposite) A scene from the play *Returning Home on a Snowy Night,* **written by Wu Zuguang, performed June 1982. Favorite of late premier Zhou Enlai, it is non-political, laden with homosexual allusions, and deals with life's inner meaning — a topic considered frivolous during the Cultural Revolution when only eight rigidly proletarian plays were sanctioned for performance. (Right) "We want artistic freedom," says the placard, echoing the plea of millions of Chinese artists and intellectuals, during a demonstration in 1979. The bearer, Wang Keping, 32, was himself once a self-righteous Red Guard, happy to denounce western art for its decadence. Today he is one of the small group of avant-garde artists in China painting and sculpting in the western style.**

143

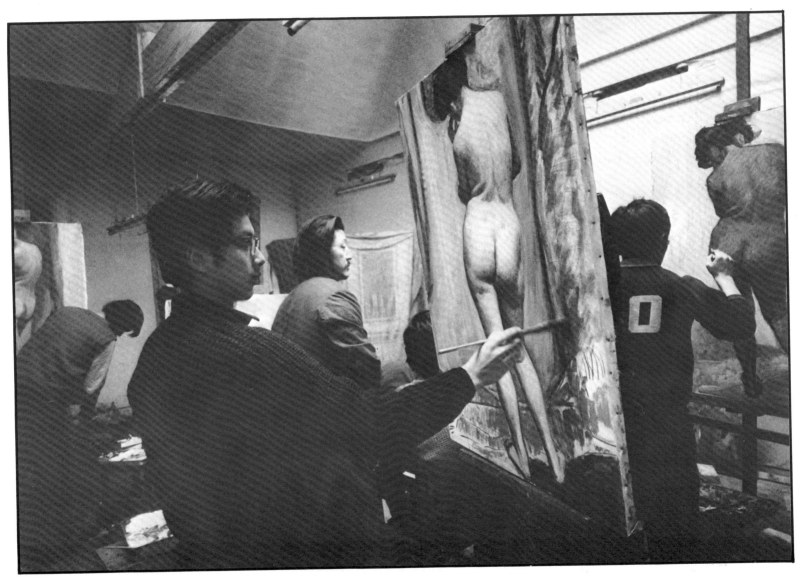

In Peking's prestigious Central Fine Arts Academy, student painters work with a live model — usually an educated, unemployed young man or woman, 1981. In the early 1950's, before it was damned as bourgeois and decadent, this was standard coursework in China's art schools.

Wang Keping surrounded by his latest sculptures, 1982. He is a full-time scriptwriter for government television, but his works have never been produced. Nowadays he seldom shows up at the studio. "I believe art should not be made to serve politics, and politics should ensure full artistic development," he says.

(Above) In a scene from the play *913,* the story of Defense Minister Lin Biao's plot to assassinate Mao, actors playing Mao and Zhou Enlai discuss strategies to counter Lin's intrigue. The Chinese stage is still unable to treat Mao as a person. Whenever he appears, make-up, lighting and sound are contrived to evoke the image of a god. (Right) Comic artists perform in a small 50-seat theater in Beihai Park. These satires, based on contemporary daily life, are for the amusement of ordinary people visiting the park. Once, theater-going was almost a political assignment. Now the performing arts are no longer dominated by strident political themes, although shows which go too far beyond reality are still sometimes shunned by the public.

Actor portrays the character of "Ah Q" during a performance in 1982. *The True Story of Ah Q* was written by one of China's greatest 20th century writers, Lu Xun (1881-1936). It is a study of the Chinese national ability — acquired through years of practice — to keep smiling in the face of adversity.

148

(Left) Author Bai Hua, 52, was branded a rightist in the anti-right campaign of 1957, and put under house arrest from 1966-73. Surviving the ordeal, he continues to write and is still published today, his case frequently stated by literary and cultural officials as an example of the country's new, more tolerant policies towards intellectuals. He is famed for his play, *Unrequited Love,* which was later made into the controversial film, *The Sun and Man,* about a Chinese painter who returns to the motherland during the Cultural Revolution only to find himself persecuted as a foreign spy. The film was vehemently attacked by conservatives, who resisted the Party's reformed policy towards intellectuals in the late 1950's. The short-lived policy, dubbed, "Let a hundred flowers blossom and a hundred schools of thought contend," was designed to woo intellectuals back and gain their confidence in the country's modernization drive. Finally, Bai Hua was labeled "anti-Party" and "anti-socialism," and the film was banned. (Right) Former union official Chen Qi, 50, reads a newspaper in his office at the *Worker's Daily* in Peking. Chen wrote an investigative report that blew the lid off a major oil rig collapse in the Bohai Gulf, which killed 72 people and caused losses totaling over 37 million yuan (19 million US dollars). The report, which exposed inept petroleum industry officials, set the precedent for a more realistic journalism in China's government-controlled press.

Woman gallery attendant takes a *xiuxi* (nap) during exhibition hour in Beihai Park Arts Gallery, 1979.

While the attendant takes her *xiuxi,* Chinese art enthusiasts study one of the paintings at the Boston Museum Exhibition, the first ever official showing of American paintings in China, in the Peking Arts Museum, 1981. At the last minute the Chinese demanded that 13 abstracts be removed. But the paintings — by Jackson Pollock, Helen Frankenthaler, Morris Louis and others — triumphed over the official censors in the end, and stayed.

(Above) Li Xiumin, 27, China's top actress of 1981, shows her own photos at home in a dormitory of the Peking Film Studio. Ms Li is well known for her authentic portrayals of Chinese peasant women. (Right) Director Ling Zifeng of Peking Film Studio on the set of *Rickshaw Boy,* 1982. Ling was criticized and denounced as a "womanizer" during the Cultural Revolution. (Opposite, left) Peking Film Studio actor Chen Qiang rests at home in 1981. In China, there are 1,000 government-employed actors and actresses and seven major film studios, which together turned out about 100 feature films in 1982. (Opposite, right) Four Peking Film Studio actresses pose for a portrait. They are all in their mid-30's and complain that the Cultural Revolution robbed them of the best years of their careers. Now they are given only minor parts in the Studio's dozen or so features a year.

Cao Yu, China's top playwright, and his wife, Li Yuru — herself a noted Peking Opera singer — in their flat in Shanghai, 1980. "We are beginning to achieve real freedom of speech in China," said Cao. Like most other writers, Cao was forced to do manual labor during the Cultural Revolution. "Maybe the younger generation was spared," he said, "but we suffered terribly."

(Right) Ding Ling, 79, China's top feminist writer, who won the Stalin award for literature in 1951. During the Cultural Revolution, she was sent as a laborer to a Chinese gulag in Heilongjiang Province. Today she deplores the "wounded literature" of China's younger writers, who question the communist system and dwell on its basic flaws. (Above) Ai Qing, 73, the so-called "Prince of Chinese poetry," writes at home in 1980. During the Cultural Revolution, he was forced to live in exile in an underground cell in the desert lands of Xinjiang. Light was scarce, and he eventually lost his eyesight in one eye. "I used to hear the steps of mules passing over my head in the desert. Each time a mule-cart went by, it showered me with dust and sand. I desperately needed light," he said.

Artists at work in Fuxing Park, Shanghai, 1977. After years of self-imposed artistic isolation in China, many artists still content themselves with paintings of Chinese landscapes, and are reluctant to risk more adventurous themes.

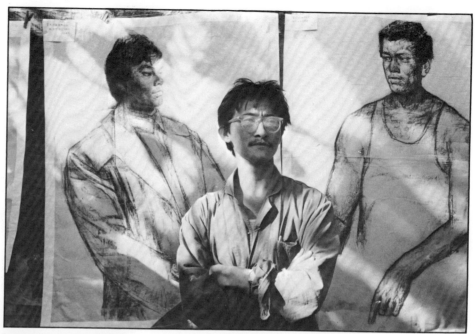

(Left) Artist Yuan Yunsheng puts finishing touches to an abstract in his classroom home in Peking's Institute of Fine Arts. Yuan painted a controversial mural for Peking's new airport of an ethnic Dai water-splashing festival showing numerous voluptuous female figures bathing in the nude. The painting caused an uproar amongst art censors who ordered Yuan to ''clothe the nudes.'' He refused, and today the bathers have been boarded up and hidden from view. (Above) Ren Zichun, 28, stands before his first exhibition of charcoal portraits strung on a clothesline at Democracy Wall, 1979. His subjects are generally construction workers on the job. Twice rejected by art schools, Ren worked as a plasterer for nine years instead. He blames his failures on his ''poor background'' and ''lack of connections.''

Members of the Shanghai Ballet perform a scene from *Swan Lake,* **Shanghai, 1981. A western choreographer commented, "The Chinese dancers have been out of practice for so long; their steps have become too hard, too mechanical."**

Zhao Yenxia, 54, prima donna of a famous Peking Opera troupe, tests herself in the mirror in a backstage dressing-room. Initiator of daring economic reforms within the group, Zhao says her troupe has discarded two of Chairman Mao's cardinal principles: the "Iron Rice Bowl" — guaranteed wages for workers and sluggards alike — and the "Big Pot" — everyone living off the group's income, whether they contribute or not.

FOREIGN FRIENDS

(Above) US Senator Howard Baker, a dedicated amateur photographer, in the Forbidden City, 1982. In 1978, China opened its doors to foreign visitors and in 1982, 1.55 million tourists passed through the country. (Opposite) "Big Bird," from the American TV show *Sesame Street,* makes his debut in China in the Workers' Palace, Peking 1982. "Big Bird" came to China to be filmed, and millions of Chinese children can now see him on Chinese television.

"We have friends all over the world," say the slogans all over China. And in opening to the West, China has seen a stream of foreign visitors reminiscent of the kings and chieftains — considered barbarians — who came to pay tribute to the emperor of the Middle Kingdom 2,000 years ago.

Heads of state, politicians, Texas oilmen, American astronauts, French fashion designers, Nobel laureates and the Harlem Globetrotters have all, at one time or another, seen the Great Wall. Cambodian Prince Norodom Sihanouk has a part-time residence and holds court in Peking. New York City Mayor Ed Koch rode the Peking subway and urged the Chinese to tear down an enormous portrait of Stalin in the central square.

French designer Pierre Cardin dressed blushing Chinese models in outlandish clothes and high-heeled shoes. US publisher Malcolm Forbes released a hot air balloon for the sheer joy of it while frantic Chinese authorities screamed futilely on the ground. Yehudi Menuhin listened far into the night to a 12 year-old violinist who had traveled all the way from the remote Xinjiang region to play for him.

But China, once subjugated by foreigners, remains suspicious of them and their ideas. Foreign technology may be necessary to China's modernization, but not so foreign values, such as bourgeois democracy, freedom of speech, free trade unions and sexual freedom.

Chinese are warned that some foreigners, especially residents, are spies and are not to be trusted. "Don't say too much, get too close or go beyond the superficial friendliness and platitudes of the tour guide," they are told. Most Chinese need permission even to have lunch with a foreigner, and inviting a foreign friend home can mean an inquiry from the police. In June 1982, an American woman, Lisa Wichser, was deported after allegations that she was a spy.

(Left) American publisher Malcolm
Forbes rides a Harley Davidson to the
Great Wall where he demonstrates the hot-
air balloon. Forbes led a team of motorcyclists from Xi'an to Peking, where he
stunned accompanying Chinese sports officials by taking off in his balloon and land-
ing in a PLA military camp. Hundreds of
soldiers surrounded the publisher, the com-
mander saluted him and a banquet was
later held in his honor in the Great Hall of
the People. To seal the friendship, Forbes
bequeathed the balloon along with three
Harley Davidsons to the Chinese, 1982.
(Above) American basketball giant Kareem
Abdul Jabbar (2.18 m) surprises the local
Moslem restaurant with a visit on a day of
fasting. In Capital Stadium, he met his
match — Han Pengshan (2.21 m).

Muhammad Ali throws a fist at the golden lion in the Forbidden City as his wife, Veronica, looks on. Ali coached the Chinese boxers at a closed session in 1981.

French designer Pierre Cardin lends a touch of class to a Chinese worker during the opening of Cardin's boutique in the Temple of Heaven Park, 1981. Cardin has staged two fashion shows in China which both charmed and dazzled his audiences. Soon he will tantalize Chinese gourmets by opening a branch of the legendary *Maxim's* **of Paris in Peking.**

Having opened the way for Sino-US rapprochement during a secret visit to China in 1971, Henry Kissinger returns to Peking in 1982 when relations between the two countries have become strained over US arms sales to Taiwan. He arrives on the eve of the 10th anniversary of the signing of the Shanghai Communiqué. China regards Kissinger as a friend, and welcomes him with open arms.

(Above) Coca Cola Chairman Robert Goizueta toasts Chinese officials with a bottle of Coke during the opening of the first Coke plant in Peking, 1981. Most Chinese find Coke either too expensive, or they object to its "medicinal" flavor. It costs 80 fen (40 US cents) a bottle — more than the average Chinese pays for a day's food. "Still," says Goizueta, "this is momentous. We now have one billion more potential consumers of Coke." (Right) Prince Norodom Sihanouk, mercurial playboy of Cambodia now living in exile in Peking, points to a portrait of himself in his villa provided by the Chinese government, 1980. Sihanouk and his beautiful wife, Princess Monique, now split most of their time between Peking and Pyongyang, North Korea. His dog was a gift from the North Korean president.

(Right) Former US President Richard Nixon poses as a waiter aboard the train from Hangzhou to Shanghai, 1982. He came to China to mark the 10th anniversary of the signing of the Shanghai Communiqué, which paved the way for normalization of Sino-US relations in 1979. (Below) French Ambassador to Peking Charles Malo waltzes with a Chinese singer from the Peking Central Philharmonic at a party to celebrate the 60th birthday of exiled Cambodian Prince Sihanouk. It was a grand occasion, fit for a king, and a rare event for Peking's diplomatic corps.

(Above) Renowned conductor Seiji Ozawa of the Boston Philharmonic rehearses *Huang He* (Song of Joy) with a powerful Chinese chorus for the first Peking performance in 20 years of Beethoven's Ninth Symphony. (Left) After the performance, Ozawa is awarded a standing ovation. (Opposite, left) Former Korean War POW, American James Dimitrios Venares, listens to a young violin student on Shandong University campus, 1981. With him is his third Chinese wife, Chen Xiumei. Before joining the war and deciding to stay in China, Venares was a laborer in Pennsylvania. He was among the few foreigners to take part in the Cultural Revolution, joining the radical faction, only to be denounced before long as a US spy. Today, he still quotes Mao with gusto. (Opposite, above) Graham Earnshaw, Peking correspondent for the *London Daily Telegraph,* sings Beatles' songs before a captivated audience in Peking's Teachers' College, 1981. Soon after the concert, China launched a campaign against bourgeois liberalism. Singing, listening and dancing to western popular music are now banned on campuses throughout China. (Opposite, below) American jazz musicians Willie Ruff and Dwight Mitchell hold an impromptu jam session in a dormitory of the Peking Conservatory, 1981. Ruff is a professor of music at Yale University and Mitchell is a professional pianist from New York City.

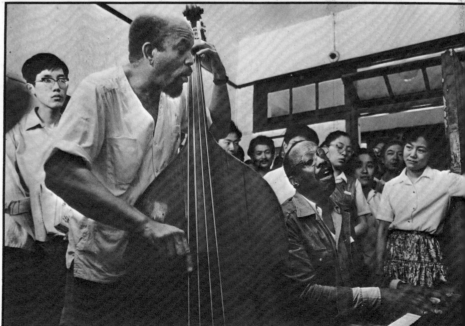

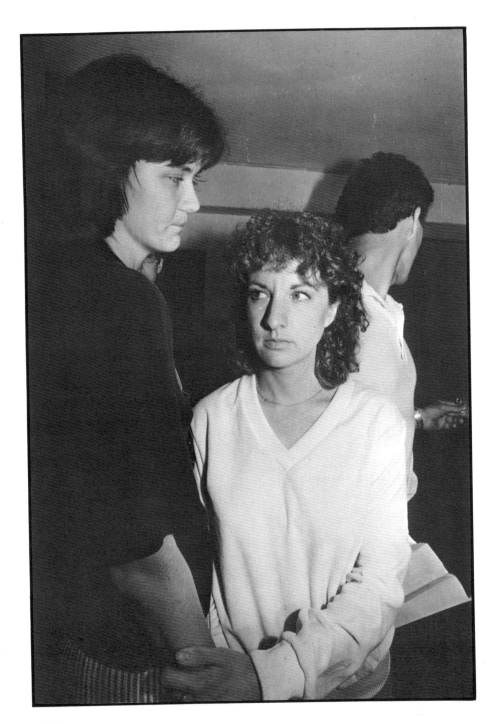

(Left) Clasping the hand of a friend for support, American PhD candidate Lisa Wichser (center) returns to her room in the Friendship Hotel to pack after her release from police detention. She was held on a charge of alleged spying, eventually expelled, and forced to leave behind her Chinese boyfriend whom she had hoped to marry. (Opposite) 74 year-old Hannah Agre, said to be the last Jew in China. She lives alone in a tiny room in a former synagogue in the city of Harbin, where she was born of Russian-Jewish parents. During the Cultural Revolution, she was stoned by the Red Guards and forced to hide her wooden Star of David under the thin mattress where it could not be found by the authorities. "My soul is so unhappy — Israel can do without me," she says. "I have lived in this room for 36 years, and I don't want to go anywhere".

In the Great Hall of the People, French Communist Party Secretary General George Marchais prepares to announce that the FCP and the CCP have resumed Party to Party relations, 1982. China has re-established Party relations with all Western European countries, and officially recognized Eurocommunism.

New York City Mayor Ed Koch comes to grips with a streetsweeper on Shanghai's Nanjing Road, 1980. Koch was impressed by the bicycle lanes in Peking and, on his return to New York, ordered special lanes marked out in the city to encourage cyclists and conserve energy.

Arts enthusiast Joan Mondale visits a temple in Foshan, Guangdong Province. Mrs Mondale accompanied her husband, former US Vice-President Walter Mondale, on an official visit to China in August 1979.

(Opposite, left) Cultural Minister Zhu Muzi (left) and Vice Foreign Minister Qian Qichen (right) celebrate the 60th anniversary of the Bolshevik Revolution with Soviet Ambassador to Peking Shcherbakov (center), 1982. China and the Soviet Union have begun consultations to improve their relations after the split of the 1960's (Opposite, right) To strengthen her position at the head of the third world, China invites and courts its leaders. Here, Libyan strongman Muammar Khadafy speaks to a Chinese interpreter at the Great Wall, during a visit in which he embarrassed his Chinese hosts by insisting on bringing his own female bodyguards dressed in combat fatigues, 1982. (Above) Deng Xiaoping steals a glance at the quintessential American capitalist, Dr Armand Hammer, 1982. The Chinese refer to Hammer — who once met with Lenin — as a "Red capitalist." He has signed a joint-venture agreement to develop the world's largest opencut coalmine in Shanxi Province.

Chinese youth puts his feet up in Peking's Beihai Park. China's new Constitution guarantees everyone the right to rest, which Chinese can take anywhere, even on ice.

PT206 148